If you have a home computer with Internet access you may:

- request an item to be placed on hold.
- renew an item that is not overdue or on hold.
- view titles and due dates checked out on your card.
- view and/or pay your outstanding fines online ($1 & over).

To view your patron record from your home computer click on Patchogue-Medford Library's homepage: www.pmlib.org

EXTREME WINTER
SPORTS ZONE

SNOWBOARD CROSS

Darice Bailer

Ŀ Lerner Publications Company • Minneapolis

Lerner Publications Company
A division of Lerner Publishing Group, Inc.
241 First Avenue North
Minneapolis, MN 55401 U.S.A.

Website address: www.lernerbooks.com

Content Consultant: Nate Deschenes, senior editor, *Snowboard Magazine*

Library of Congress Cataloging-in-Publication Data
Bailer, Darice.
    Snowboard cross / by Darice Bailer.
        pages   cm. — (Extreme winter sports zone)
    Includes index.
    ISBN 978–1–4677–0755–8 (lib. bdg. : alk. paper)
    ISBN 978–1–4677–1733–5 (eBook)
    1. Snowboarding—Juvenile literature. 2. Snocross—Juvenile literature. I. Title.
GV857.S57B34 2014
796.939—dc23   2013003025

Manufactured in the United States of America
1—PP—7/15/13

The images in this book are used with the permission of: © Philippe Millereau/DPPI/Icon SMI, 5; © GEPA/Imago/Icon SMI, 6; © LORENVU/DPPI-SIPA/Icon SMI, 7, 15; © Courtney Crow/Sport the Library/Icon SMI, 8; © Jed Conklin/Zuma Press/Icon SMI, 9; © Armando Trovat/AP Images, 10; © Whitehead/AP Images, 11; © Andrey Artykov/Alamy, 12; © sainthorant daniel/Shutterstock Images, 13; © Mike Powell/Getty Images, 14; © Daniel Petty/Denver Post/AP Images, 16; © Doug Pensinger/Getty Images, 17, 20; © Jean-Christophe Bott/Keystone/AP Images, 18; © Clément Allard, CP/AP Images, 19; © Mark Carlson/AP Images, 21; © Rick Bowmer/AP Images, 22; © Charles Taylor/Shutterstock Images, 23; © mountainpix/Shutterstock Images, 24–25, 28, 29; © Vito Zgonc/Shutterstock Images, 26; © Paman Aheri/Shutterstock Images, 27; Philippe Millereau/ DPPI/Icon SMI, 28.

Front cover: © Doug Pensinger/Getty Images; backgrounds: © kcv/Shutterstock.com.

Main body text set in Folio Std Light 11/17.
Typeface provided by Adobe Systems.

TABLE OF CONTENTS

CHAPTER ONE

OLYMPIC DREAMS

Americans Nate Holland and Seth Wescott gripped the starting gate. It was February 15, 2010. The two friends and teammates were getting ready to speed down the mountain. Holland and Wescott could hear the crowd cheering. Seconds later, the gate in front of them dropped. The pair exploded out of the gate and onto the course alongside two other Olympians. The adventure was on!

MAKING THE FINALS

The Olympic snowboard cross event starts with 32 racers. These racers compete in qualifying races called heats. Each heat has four snowboarders. The top two racers in each heat advance until the group is whittled down to eight. From there the four snowboarders with the fastest times move on to the final race. They have a chance to win a gold, silver, or bronze medal.

Seth Wescott hoped
to win his second gold
medal in snowboard
cross at the 2010 Winter
Olympic Games.

The four men's snowboard cross finalists soar off a jump, with Mike Robertson in the lead.

Holland and Wescott were competing in the men's snowboard cross finals at the 2010 Winter Olympic Games in Vancouver, British Columbia. In this fast-paced race, shredders (snowboarders) speed down a long, narrow course. The path is different for every event. But snowboard cross courses usually have similar features, such as kickers (jumps), rollers (bumps), and sharp turns. The Olympic course wound its way 4,035 feet (1,230 meters) to the finish. That is 0.8 miles (1.3 kilometers). The race would be over in less than one minute and 20 seconds.

Canada's Mike Robertson won the hole shot. This meant he grabbed the lead into the first icy turn. Holland was in second place. France's Tony Ramoin was in third. Wescott was at the back of the pack.

Soon Wescott caught up. He and Holland were neck and neck into the first set of rollers. The two friends chased their gold medal dreams down the mountain.

The pack sped more than 40 miles (64 km) per hour down the course. Holland worked hard to catch up to Robertson. Holland soared over the next jump elbow to elbow with the Canadian. With a thump, the pair landed and sped on.

Snowboard cross is one of the most dangerous sports at the Winter Olympic Games. Riders often bump into one another at high speeds. In an earlier round, at least one rider in each heat had spun out or crashed.

Crashes are common in snowboard cross. At the 2006 Winter Olympic Games in Turin, Italy, U.S. snowboarder Lindsey Jacobellis lost her lead when she crashed during the women's snowboard cross finals.

Warm temperatures and rain had melted some of the snow on the course. Holland hit a hole. He lost his balance and spun out of control. His race was over. It looked as though Robertson would win the gold medal.

But Wescott wasn't done yet. He crouched low in a tight ball. Then he whipped over the next jump. He flew past Ramoin. Wescott was chasing down Robertson for the lead.

On the second-to-last jump before the final big turn, Wescott was head-to-head with Robertson. The pair was just 20 seconds away from the finish line. Wescott knew this was his last chance to win the race.

Wescott and Robertson soar over the last jump of the 2010 Olympic men's snowboard cross finals.

Wescott bent his knees and flew over the jump. He passed Robertson in the air. Wescott landed solidly. He hung on to his small lead around the final turn and over the last jump. When he crossed the finish line first, Wescott raised his arms. He had won by one length of a board. The gold medal was his!

Wescott (center) won the gold medal in men's snowboard cross, Robertson (left) took silver, and Ramoin (right) won bronze at the 2010 Olympic Games.

CHAPTER TWO
HISTORY OF SNOWBOARD CROSS

People started snowboarding long before the first riders raced down snowboard cross courses. In 1917 a 13-year-old Minnesota boy named Vern Wicklund created a sled he stood up on while riding. He and his friends called the sled a bunker. In 1939 Wicklund and two relatives patented a similar stand-up sled. These early snowboards were made out of oak. They weighed at least 15 pounds (6.8 kilograms).

In New Jersey in 1963, 12-year-old Tom Sims carved a board he could use to go down hills. It worked like a skateboard in the snow. Tom called his creation a skiboard. Two years later, a

Snowboarding is a relatively new sport.

Surfers inspired early snowboard designers.

Michigan businessman named Sherman Poppen bolted two skis together. He and his family used the device to surf down a hill in his backyard. Poppen called his invention the Snurfer. Soon the Snurfer was being sold as a toy.

A New Design

In the early 1970s, a surfer named Dimitrije Milovich began designing boards that would work like surfboards on snow. He developed two models of the snow surfboard and began selling them under the name Winterstick. Milovich's Wintersticks were featured in magazines, bringing new attention to the young sport. But Milovich had a hard time selling his invention to bigger stores. He eventually had to close down his business.

BOARDER TALK
Boosted: flew much higher than normal
Slash: spray snow

In 1977 Jake Burton began thinking of ways to improve the Snurfer. He had first tried the Snurfer at the age of 14. Burton loved riding it. He thought it could be more than a toy. Burton added bindings to keep his feet attached to the board. He called his invention a snowboard. Soon he had started his own company, Burton Snowboards. These improved boards would be used in a brand-new sport.

Snowboarding Takes Off

At first it was hard for the new sport to find a home. Ski resorts were afraid that snowboarders would crash into skiers. Burton begged ski resorts to let shredders ride his new snowboard on their hills. In 1982 Burton invited a few snowboarders to the first National Snowboarding

Early snowboards looked much different from the boards modern snowboard cross stars use.

Championships (later called the U.S. Open Snowboarding Championships). The event took place in Vermont. The starting gate was just an upside-down table. Snowboard boots did not exist yet. The winner wore sneakers while hurtling 63 miles (101 km) per hour down the steep hill.

In 1991 Steven Rechtschaffner and Greg Stump created an eight-episode television series about extreme sports. Stump hosted the series, which was called *Greg Stump's World of Extremes*. The pair needed a daredevil sport to film for the final episode.

Rechtschaffner had an idea. In a popular sport called motocross, motorcyclists raced on a dirt course with steep bumps and sharp turns. Why not combine motocross with snowboarding? This would create a challenging trail for snowboarders to race down. The first racer over the finish line would win. The new event would be called boardercross.

The first snowboard cross event was inspired by motocross races, which are popular events during summer months.

The first boardercross race took place in April 1991. The course was built on Blackcomb Mountain in British Columbia. Eight snowboarders shot down a course with seven jumps and five tight turns. Everyone had a blast. The show was a hit. People couldn't wait to ride down a course themselves. Boardercross was so popular that Rechtschaffner filled out papers to trademark the name. Owning the trademark for boardercross meant no one else could call a snowboard event by that name without Rechtschaffner's permission.

But that didn't stop races from happening. The sport was popular with young people. ESPN included it in the very first Winter X Games extreme sports competition in 1997. ESPN called its event Snowboarder X.

A SPORT WITH MANY NAMES

The Winter Olympics calls their snowboard-racing competition snowboard cross. But different events have different names for the sport. ESPN calls the event Snowboarder X at the Winter X Games. If that isn't confusing enough, many snowboarders use a different name when talking about the sport they love. These shredders call the sport by its original name—boardercross!

The Winter X Games had the biggest competition in snowboard racing. Athletes traveled from all over the world to compete. Then, in 2006, snowboard cross debuted at the 2006 Olympic Games in Turin, Italy. No matter what people called it, the young sport was a success!

torino 200

Switzerland's Tanja Frieden (left) and U.S. shredder Lindsey Jacobellis (right) race for the gold medal in women's snowboard cross at the 2006 Winter Olympics.

CHAPTER THREE

AWESOME COMPETITIONS

For many years, the Winter X Games were the biggest event in snowboard cross. About 35 million Americans turned on the TV to watch the Winter X Games in 2012. Many of these fans watched Nate Holland win the snowboard cross gold medal. This was Holland's fifth Winter X gold medal in snowboard cross. Then the snowboard world was shocked when the Winter X Games canceled their snowboard cross competition for 2013. One reason may have been the

Nate Holland (right, center) is in the lead as a group of snowboard cross racers clear a jump on Buttermilk Mountain at the 2012 Winter X Games.

U.S. snowboarder Nick Baumgartner starts a training run on the snowboard cross course at the 2012 Sprint U.S. Grand Prix.

expense. It costs a lot to build the complex course with jumps and turns. Fortunately, there are many other competitions where snowboard cross shredders can show off their skills.

The Winter Olympic Games are held every four years. Countries around the world send their best athletes to race in snowboard cross to compete in the games.

Each year the U.S. National Championships, also known as the Sprint U.S. Grand Prix, bring the best U.S. shredders together. The top man and woman each win a green dinner jacket and prize money.

ROOKIES RACING LEGENDS

Each year a competition in Washington brings together shredders of all levels and snowboarding styles. The race is called the Mount Baker Legendary Banked Slalom. A slalom is a zigzag race marked by flags. Winners receive a roll of gold, silver, or bronze duct tape. The duct tape prize is because snowboarders didn't always use real snowboard boots or bindings. Riders once wrapped tape around their regular snow boots to stiffen them for riding. Some riders even duct-taped their boots to their snowboards.

Canada's Dominique Maltais competes at a 2012 race in Switzerland.

FIS Events

The International Ski Federation (FIS) hosts Snowboard World Cups around the world each year. These races include individual and team competitions. The World Cups give the best pro snowboarders a chance to race against one another. Every course is different. Racers usually compete in heats of four or six snowboarders. The top 30 finishers at each World Cup receive points. The winner receives the most points. These points go toward the world ranking. When the season ends, the male and female with the most points is named World Champion. These two athletes are awarded a crystal globe trophy and prize money. FIS also holds competitions for the best junior snowboarders around the world.

The U.S. Ski and Snowboard Association (USSA) was founded in 1905. Young snowboard cross racers compete in different age groups. The Hole Shot Cross Tour is a group of events where young snowboarders can race against one another. Some young racers may catch the eye of a national coach. Juniors have the chance to ride with some of the best snowboarders in the country on the U.S. Revolution Tour.

Each spring the top four junior boys and girls from the Hole Shot Cross and Revolution tours are invited to train with top coaches for a week. Some of these teens just might become the next Olympians.

Canadian snowboarder Drew Neilson celebrates after winning the 2007 crystal globe trophy in snowboard cross.

19

CHAPTER FOUR

GET ON BOARD

The road to becoming a professional snowboarder isn't easy. It takes a lot of time, talent, and training. Snowboard cross racer Hagen Kearney started snowboarding when he was just nine years old. He grew up watching Nate Holland win the Winter X Games. It wasn't long before Kearney joined a local snowboard club in Telluride, Colorado. He began racing on weekends. Kearney attended a snowboard summer camp. At the camp, he learned how to snowboard better, faster, and safer.

The hard work doesn't stop once a snowboarder makes it to the top level. In 2012 Kearney made the U.S. Snowboard Cross B Team. This

Hagen Kearney is an up-and-coming snowboard cross racer.

The U.S. Ski and Snowboard Team trains year-round at the Center of Excellence in Park City, Utah.

team is for talented racers who aren't quite ready to be members of the U.S. Ski and Snowboard Team. But Kearney still got to train with the top team. Members of both teams train at the Center of Excellence in Park City, Utah. Off the snow, Kearney and the other athletes work out in the gym.

TEAM RACING

Kearney got the chance to team up with Holland, his childhood hero, during a snowboard cross team race at the 2012 Snowboard Cross World Cup in Montafon, Austria. At the race, Kearney sped down the hill first. When he reached the finish line, a sensor triggered the gate to open for Holland back at the top. The first team to get both racers across the finish line would win. Kearny and Holland were quick enough to take first in the event.

Snowboard Camps

Kearney had the right idea. Snowboard cross is a dangerous sport. Even professional shredders fall. Rookie snowboarders need safe and careful coaching to learn the sport properly. Snowboard camps like the one Kearney attended are great ways to introduce new shredders to snowboard cross.

Windells in Mount Hood, Oregon, is a famous camp that brings in the best snowboard coaches to teach beginners. These talented coaches help develop future snowboard cross stars. Even U.S. Olympic snowboard coach Mike Jankowski has worked with kids at Windells.

Stratton Mountain Resort in Vermont hosts the Heavy Medal Boardercross Camp. Olympic medalists Ross Powers and Lindsey Jacobellis coach at this camp. At Heavy Medal, beginners between the ages of 10 and 18 learn the techniques they need to tear up a course.

Snowboard cross camps teach young shredders snowboarding skills. They learn how to speed out of the starting gate. Young snowboarders discover how to pick the best and fastest path down the mountain. Many camps give beginners the chance to meet famous racers and coaches. Beginners also learn important safety tips. But before hitting the snow, shredders need to make sure they have the right safety gear.

TAKING CARE OF A SNOWBOARD

Pro snowboard cross racers wax their snowboards every couple of days to keep them in good shape. Wax helps a board glide more smoothly over the snow. Most pros wax their boards right before a race. First, they drip the wax on with a special iron. Then they carefully use the iron to melt the wax onto the board. Once the wax is cool, it's time to scrape it off with a scraper. Finally, shredders use a brush to rub off any leftover wax.

Pro snowboard cross racers wax their boards before big races. Using the right wax for the outside temperature helps a snowboard move more quickly.

SUPER
SNOWBOARD CROSS
GEAR

BOOTS

Boots are important for steering and control. Racers use stiff boots designed for snowboarding. Snowboard cross boots should be snug but comfortable.

PADS

Think of pads as body bumpers. Ski shops sell padded shorts or pants to protect a snowboarder's hips, knees, and tailbone. Padded tops and forearm and elbow pads also cushion a fall.

HELMET

Wearing a helmet is very important in snowboard cross. Helmets help protect athletes' brains from serious injury. Some pros, such as Lindsey Jacobellis, wear a motocross helmet. This style of helmet covers her entire face.

JACKET, PANTS, AND GLOVES

Snowboard cross races often take place in cold and windy weather. Racers need to be prepared for the elements with warm jackets, pants, and gloves. Most racers wear pants and jackets that aren't too baggy. Loose clothing catches the air, slowing racers down.

GOGGLES

A good pair of goggles helps block the sun's harmful rays. They also protect a racer's eyes from wind and snow. Good goggles won't fog up, scratch, or shatter. The strap needs to be big enough to fit over the helmet.

SNOWBOARD

Snowboard cross boards are a little bigger than normal snowboards. They are also a lot stiffer. This design helps a racer stay steady while hurtling along bumps and around turns. Pros wax their snowboards before competitions to give them an extra edge.

Snowboard cross racer and Winter X Games medalist Alexandra Jekova wore the right safety gear at a race in 2012.

It's important to find a place with few people around to practice snowboarding. That way new shredders won't risk injuring other snowboarders or skiers.

Hitting the Snow

Snowboard camps can be expensive. But kids can start learning the techniques for snowboard cross anywhere there's snow. Rookies should find a place that's not too crowded to practice. They need to stay away from other snowboarders or sledders. Then beginners can try racing to the bottom of a straight hill.

Once they are comfortable snowboarding down a small hill, shredders can take their skills to a terrain park at a ski resort. Terrain parks have rails and kickers that snowboarders use for tricks. Shredders can practice tucking their bodies over the jumps. Tucking the body is an important skill for snowboard cross racers. Racers need to be tight and compact to fly over jumps quickly. Racers should get down low by bending at the waist and knees. They should keep their arms close to their bodies. Then the racers just need to stay low, spot the landing, and touch down safely.

Even if there's no snow around, snowboard cross racers can practice their skills by hopping on skateboards. Stars like Wescott and Kearney are known for their skateboarding skills. Skateboarding helps get athletes in shape before hitting the slopes. Being fit and healthy is very important in snowboard racing.

Even if you never make it into the snowboard cross race, snowboarding is a great way to get outside in the winter. Just remember to have fun and stay safe!

Skateboarding is a great way for shredders to stay in shape during the warmer months.

SNOWBOARD STARS

SETH WESCOTT

Seth Wescott grew up in Maine. He started out as a downhill skier. But he started snowboarding in 1986 when he was 10 years old. He was so talented that Burton Snowboards sponsored him when he was just 13. Wescott later pushed to get snowboard cross into the Olympic Games. His hard work paid off. Wescott won back-to-back gold medals at the 2006 and 2010 Winter Olympic Games. He also won three silver medals in snowboard cross at the Winter X Games between 2002 and 2010.

NATE HOLLAND

Snowboarder Nate Holland learned to ski near his home in Idaho when he was three years old. Soon he learned how to skateboard too. On his 10th birthday in 1988, Holland begged his parents for a snowboard. At the age of 12, Holland started competing. In 2004 *Ski Racing Magazine* named Holland Boardercross Racer of the Year. In 2010 Holland set a Winter X Games record by winning his fifth straight gold medal in snowboard cross. Holland's gold streak stopped with a bronze medal in 2011. But he came back to win gold in snowboard cross in 2012.

MAELLE RICKER

Canadian snowboarder Maelle Ricker grew up in North Vancouver, British Columbia, snowboard racing with her older brother. Ricker turned pro after finishing high school in June 1996. She won gold medals in snowboarder cross at the Winter X Games in 1999 and 2006. She also won the gold medal in snowboard cross at the 2010 Winter Olympic Games. In 2011 Ricker was inducted into the British Columbia Sports Hall of Fame.

LINDSEY JACOBELLIS

Snowboarder Lindsey Jacobellis grew up in Vermont. She began snowboard racing when she was 11 years old. She won a silver medal in snowboard cross at the 2006 Olympic Games. And she finished in fifth place at the 2010 Winter Olympic Games. Jacobellis has won the gold medal in snowboard cross at the Winter X Games seven times between 2003 and 2011.

GLOSSARY

AMATEUR

someone who participates in an activity for fun without expectation of payment

HEAT

qualifying race

HOLE SHOT

the first racer to the first turn in a snowboard cross race

KICKER

small jump

PROFESSIONAL

someone who participates in an activity as a job for payment

ROLLER

a small bump

ROOKIE

someone who is new to a sport or activity

SHRED

to snowboard

FOR MORE INFORMATION

Further Reading

Bailer, Darice. *Snowboard Superpipe*. Minneapolis: Lerner Publications Company, 2014.

Kleh, Cindy. *Being a Snowboarder*. Minneapolis: Lerner Publications Company, 2012.

———. *Snowboarding Skills: The Back-to-Basics Essentials for All Levels*. Richmond Hill, ON: Firefly Books, 2002.

Websites

Safety Tips: Snowboarding
http://kidshealth.org/teen/safety/sports_safety/safety_snowboarding.html
Learn some key ways to stay safe while snowboarding.

The United States of America Snowboard Association
http://www.usasa.org
The USASA has snowboard cross races for different age groups in many regions of the country. The website provides information about these amateur races.

U.S. Snowboarding Team
http://ussnowboarding.com
The USSA offers snowboard cross programs and competitions for young athletes. Visit this website for the latest news about U.S. Ski and Snowboard Team events and winners.

INDEX

About the Author

Darice Bailer has written many books for children. She won the Parents' Choice Gold Award for her first book, *Puffin's Homecoming*. She began her career as a sports reporter and is especially fond of writing about sports for kids. She lives in Connecticut with her husband.

discard
etc